A SOUL'S JOURNEY

BY

Mary Young Olitzky

To
Joshua David
My son and teacher

Cover design by
Amanda Johnson Studios

Dear Reader,

You are about to share in a most exciting adventure of my life. A time when all my thoughts about life changed. As my thoughts changed, everything I knew in my world changed. It was a time of great joy and great pain that opened the way for new beginnings.

This is the journey of the soul that we search for and find in our own way and time.

My wish for you is that you will find in the pages of this book insights you can use on your life journey.

Enjoy the journey!

Contents

AT 19

At 19 she thought the world was hers,
Full of promise and hope and love.

She ran away with him, her love.
--My love does it good—

Gotta get away, lose myself.
Need a better life.

Party, drink, have fun, sex.
That's it. Isn't it?

Looking, searching, I know it's here somewhere.

Drink some more…feel good.
No pain.

I sit motionless. I can't move. I'm paralyzed.
--Mama told me not to come—

The voices in my head stop
I hurt too much, just love me

I'll do anything for him.

--Everybody get together, try to love one another
right now--

It's quiet now
I sit and wait
Yoga takes me to myself-Hello

Who am I

In the mirror I see his face
Yes, there is someone there
I don't want to be alone
Anybody, anybody, even you

My soul is black and empty
At least I have one

The car door slams
He demands
I am afraid
No, no more
I feel my head hit the wall
I feel weak and afraid

I'm not awake
This must be a nightmare
Oh God, please no more
I want to wake up
A drink takes away my pain
Or does it?

Michigan 1973

7

My love for you goes unrequited,
Only to be heard on silent nights…
When I call out your name.

1977

She called it the Dark Night of the Soul
I've been there and you know it's Dark.

I pray that my time will never come
To go that way again.

But having been there I feel lucky
To have come back unburdened.

Many don't survive, you know,
But the joke's on them.

Cut short their passages
And they'll be back another time.

But for today I'm here and I'm alive.

ODE TO DOUGLAS

I wish I had the words to say,
How deeply you touched me today.

Of all the men I've ever loved,
This love is of a different kind.

It's kind like you, and caring too.

The time we spend goes by so fast,
And I'm just hoping this will last.
It will if I can stay out of the past.

You say you love me and I fear,
You'll go away.
Please don't go dear.

Stay and let me love you, too.

November 1990

THE GIFT OF LOVE

The gift of love is what is special.

That wonderful gift I give myself first
Then share with others.

It is a simple gift wrapped in warmth and caring.

Sometimes wrapped in someone's arms as a hug.
And sometimes in a smile
That sends love to another across the room.

Or in the special, simple, loving actions of my love.

I give myself a warm bath or a cup of tea.
A home that feels safe to me.

March 1991

THE CHOREOGRAPHER

Oh, my body,
My supple lovely body
It is a wonder, created from love.
And my woman's body gives life
Oh wondrous form. .

I gaze at my body
Seeing all its lines and flaws
But, no—it is perfect
Co-created with God
To live life—breathe.

I feel my heart pound in my chest
Oh, sign of life.
My blood runs freely through my body
And nourishes each cell.

My body knows
It reproduces cells that no longer live,
It knows what to do.
I never have to think about
All those life signs.

My body is mine to enjoy, look at and admire
In all its splendor.
Every inch a woman.

Feeling the currents
That run through my body, sensual curves
And all parts dance this beautiful dance together.
What choreography!

My sexual parts—
How beautiful they are,
Pleasure seekers,
Where I leave my mind behind
To travel to places unknown,
To feel, just feel.

The wind caresses my naked body
It is soft and feels cool and lovely.

And my body dances its dance.

I am the choreographer.

March 1991

GOODBYE

I now divorce you from my soul
That's where our connection really was

It is so sad, but I have to let you go

We have other lessons to learn you and I
Other lives to live

There were so many magic moments
Like snapshots in my mind

Our honeymoon
When our son was born
Our first house, our second house

Moves—changes—
Nothing stays the same

And finally, I came to the fork in the road
Do I choose me or you
Funny that I stop to think

My journey takes me on a different path
Our paths never cross again in this life.

Goodbye, with love.

My old behaviors beckon to me
Like a dress in a store window

I try them on for fit, they don't anymore

I am sad and happy all at once

My little girl behaviors—so comfortable, so familiar
No longer fit me—a woman in body and spirit

I am fully awake and aware—the nightmare is over

I am healing and becoming the strong woman
God has always meant me to be

September 1991

THE MIRROR OF LOVE

I gaze into your eyes,
And contemplate the last 12 months

One year…

The fears…
The tears…
The cheers…

Love is like a mirror for you and me,
Me and you

The memories are sweet,
And sweeter still to come

You opened your heart,
And I came in to stay awhile

I am safe and warm in your loving arms

I opened my heart, too
And with that all the possibilities

For love and life

STEP ASIDE GOD

I see so clearly where you are

Follow me, I know the way

I know the ropes

You see, I've been there

I wake up with a start

And I see God watching over me

I know that your God is watching over you

I never was much good at playing God

I am relieved

I continue my journey directed only by God

August 1991

SACRED SPACE

In the quiet of the morning, I listen to my soul
It's me, the Real me, the place where God and angels go.

Life isn't always easy, it isn't always sane,
But when I go within to God, it's like coming home again.

My path lies ahead of me, most of it I cannot see,
But inch-by-inch and step-by-step more is revealed to me.

I choose to do God's will today even though I may not know,
The wonderment and miracles my life does truly hold.

I find myself in doubt at times not knowing where God's been,
And then I watch a sunrise that's the most beautiful I've seen.

The lesson here is in God's love and knowing he will provide,
My every need, want and desire without my foolish pride.

When I seek my God inside.

COME WITHIN

Come to a sacred place with me
Where I invite you into my spirit

Sit a while
While our spirits commune

I am so much like you
I am you and you are me

When another cries out in pain
I hurt

When one is joyous
I feel the happiness

Come in and be with all of me
Fear has left me

I trust the universe

We already knew each other
Before we met this time

I am here for you and with you

You say, "What does it matter?"
It matters to this ONE

May 1991

I accept myself as I am

I am a woman
Lifegiver, creator and vessel of power

My inner light shines on through generations

Children,
Grandchildren
Great grandchildren,
Genetic codes carry the message

Heal your life by finding your inner light

Once found, I shine on
My light illuminates everyone it touches

Hearts, bodies, and minds—all feeling

And all together this energy flows through me

I cannot name it, only claim it as
LOVE

April 1991

LIFE

Life is an opportunity

Some opportunities are for yes

Some opportunities are for no

Therein lies all substance of life and change

Growth and development

You and me

April 1991

FERTILE WOMAN'S LAMENT

I am pregnant again in my head
Worse than morning sickness, and I know

But, Oh, last night we had so much fun
We did use birth control,
But somehow I don't trust it will work
It has so far, 'til now that is

My head dislikes being pregnant
It's really quite negative—
Always thinking, thinking, thinking,
"What will happen then?"
No one really knows

Why don't men have to worry about these things

Single woman, unemployed, mom, career woman
Supermom, lover

Babies, formula, diapers, up all night, crying,
Pediatricians, strollers, car seats

My mind says the real question is
Do I have this baby?
I do have choices you know
But the choices are hard for me

It's time for this baby of my mind to rest
And dream of hills like white elephants

THE OTHER FLORIDA

The pungent smell of orange blossoms fill the air

Everything is blue and green

Miles upon miles of sun-kissed earth

Goddess gifts all

I am connected to the earth—the goddess smiles on me

I am alone and happy

April 1992

Our love fades, as the rose
Whose petals fall from the bloom

My tears fall like rain
To nourish the seed of new growth

An autumn chill is in my body
Echoing the loneliness from deep within

The seeds are planted

I will survive the cold, dead winter
To blossom again in the spring

Like the rose reaching toward the sun
For warmth and strength

Bursting forth in radiant beauty

What a beautiful gift for self and others to behold

It is dark and cold inside
I have been expelled from the womb

Only to find myself in this hostile place
Surrounded by quiet darkness

Death stalks me in the night
I cannot see the Enemy, but I feel it here

They're waving goodbye, bittersweet friends of fear
Lost souls to themselves

I cannot bear the weight
I cut the cord and set them adrift

I am suspended in the night
Terrified
Lonely
Alone

A few stars shine for me
I have not lost hope

I can see the light glowing, burning in my memory

How long 'til I get there—Oh it's the journey

I fasten my seat belt for the ride

The passion of woman is largely undiscovered

Waiting to burst forth when we explore

I hold mine in my heart
Where it burns with a warm glow

Be nice
Be sweet
Be a lady

They mustn't know your passion
The heat is too intense and they'll melt

Or maybe I will

I am ready to open my heart
And set the brilliance of my passion free

Some will be blinded by the light
Others will put on sunglasses, blinders

But I welcome the ones who will come close
With open hearts

Together we will dance in the light of JOY

January 1992

The sun came out today
Right in the middle of winter

I welcome it
And bask in the warmth of the sun

The winters of my life
Are brightened with sunlit moments
I capture those warm moments in my heart

My heart is open, loving and gentle
I let in those who are also loving
And appreciate my gentleness

I own my gentle spirit that nurtures my soul

I surround myself with spirits of like mind
Whose gentleness washes over me
Like the spring rain

The seasons change and new life bursts forth

In my recovery I thought I would be perfect

Not yet

In my recovery I thought situations would be perfect

Not now

In my recovery I thought you would be perfect

Not quite

I found recovery—that's perfect

Life changes as the seasons in God's perfect universe.

January 1992

Part of me has died

I am sad, confused, angry

You said you would be there,

You weren't

You lied

The lie is so familiar I don't notice

But inside that part dies

I carry it around with me

Painting a smile on my face

I hurt

I hurt

I hurt too much to pretend

October 1991

I feel a cold wind blowing around my body

Our souls have been torn apart

Where are you?

I picture your house in my mind

You're not there

I miss you

The pain goes down to my toes

Why does this have to be?

I love you

My body aches for you

My heart is broken

How can it mend?

October 1991

The river of life stretches out in front of me like a snake

Winding and curving and waiting to surprise me

The snake crawls up my spine energizing me

But, oh, sometimes he strikes a nerve

I feel like I will die

Not yet,
I can't go,
I'm not done

The snake smiles and slithers on

                              April 1992

Where did you go

You were from that other life, that other time

I know you were real, my heart glows when

I think of you

What happened to us

You and me

We grew apart

Two spirits in the cosmic fire burning

Into each other's memories

The flame still glows

Dying embers

July 1992

I remember your smile

Your voice

Your smell and taste

You are still here

Always a part of me

I bless you on your journey

And cherish our time then and again

July 1992

THERE'S GOD IN THEM THARE HILLS

There's God in them thare hills
I saw him from the top

He spoke to me from the lush green valleys and
Hazy blue mountains
I knew he was there

And when I climbed to the top over pitfalls
And slippery places
He was there

At times I almost lost my footing—I slipped back
But He said keep going, have faith, you'll make it

I wanted to quit, to sit down and cry
To scream across the valley—I can't, I won't
He just smiled and said you can make it

So I kept going, putting one foot in front of the other
One step at a time

And God walked next to me, my partner in life
I think I'm going to make it
Unless my tennis shoes wear slap out

July 1992

THE WAITING

In the quiet I hear the pulse of life

A strange journey with few distractions from the self

A contentment as yet unknown

Of piercing blue eyes and unanswered questions

Risking all that has passed before

Disconnected from the trivial,
Where the vacuum has yet to be filled

With pregnant expectations for
The adventurous morsel of juicy life
Waiting for fulfillment

To tap into a precious moment's ecstasy
Vestal virgin of life

And again, to rest and wait

The quiet pounding in my head
Knowing the moment will come

Relinquishing all control to the universe

The waiting

July 1997

THE JOURNEY

I am a traveler
Going the distance with joy, sadness and excitement

Come with me my friend
There are adventures to discover

Filled with cliffs and valleys, lush vegetation
Barren sands, and deep blue oceans

The journey is the destination
For I know not where the road will end

So travel with me my friend and go the distance

March 2021

ACKNOWLEDGEMENTS

Thank you to my wonderful friends and family who have shared and supported me on my journey. Special thanks to Bill Freeman, Tricia Youngs, Rosemary Quirin, Ling List and others too numerous to name here. You know who you are! I am so blessed to have you!

A special thanks to Amanda Johnson from Amanda Johnson Studio, my amazing artist friend who produced the cover artwork.

A big thank you to Emily Casey with La Palma Creative for helping me to get this book published. Your help was invaluable!!

Thanks to Brandi Image Photography for the back cover photo.

Thank you to all the readers of my poetry book.

Enjoy your journey!

Made in the USA
Middletown, DE
03 September 2024

60255937R00022